STRIVING TO BE THE AUTHENTIC ME

Striving To Be The Authentic Me

By Clarence T. Brown

This Book is Published By CJC Enterprise

Front Cover Design © By Olson Richardson

Copyright © 2013
All rights reserved. No part of this book may be reproduced in any form whatsoever, whether digitally or in print, without express written permission of the author except for brief quotations in critical reviews or articles.

Striving To Be The Authentic Me

www.clarencetbrown.com

Library of Congress Control Number: 2013901538
ISBN- 978-0-9802217-7-0

Printed in the United States of America

clarence@clarencetbrown.com

January 2013

Acknowledgements

As I begin writing the third installment to my Radical line, I want to say thank you to some people who have contributed to my success. I would first like to thank my **Lord and Savior Jesus Christ**, who continues to guide my actions and reveal my purpose.

To my wife **Consuela**, thank you for bearing with me as I bounce ideas off of you to perfect what I put on paper.

To **Clarence T. Brown, III**, my junior publicist and number one fan. Thanks for encouraging me to keep doing this.

To my other mother **Elester Middleton**, you are a wealth of support. Your 'my big boy can do anything mentality' keeps me going even when I want to quit.

To **Trevin Green,** thank you for being my sounding board and always keeping me on point.

To Kristen NeEma Gaither-Thompson, thank you for pushing me to continue to write.

To No Platitudes Please, LLC for the editing services. You are awesome, thank you.

To everyone that purchased my first two books, *Radical Introductions*, thank you for the support, here we go again.

CB

Contents

Foreword	ix
Disclaimer	xiv
Preface	1
Introduction	5
Chapter 1: Purpose	9
Chapter 2: The Internal Compass	19
Chapter 3: Choices	31
Chapter 4: Gravitate	47
Chapter 5: Tic-Toc, Tic-Toc, Life Clock	57
Chapter 6: Never Compromise	65
Conclusion	73
Author Profile	77

Foreword

Questions To Ponder Before You Begin This Book:

1. *Where do you see yourself in five, ten or twenty years?*
2. *If you could do or be anything, what would it be?*
3. *What are YOUR dreams?*
4. *What are YOUR goals in life?*
5. *What are YOU doing to achieve them...DAILY?*

"Go confidently in the direction of your dreams. Live the life YOU'VE imagined."
-Thoreau

    I had the pleasure of meeting Mr. Clarence T. Brown, or Friend as I refer to him now, my second year of junior-high school (8th grade) some 18 years ago. The first two questions he asked were not out of the ordinary, but they've sent me on a journey to discover who I am and what I want for MY life. I say want because the journey is never really complete, there are just more roads to explore.

ix

The simple questions were, "Who are you and what do you want to be?"

For many of us, the answers to those questions are so entwined that we lose sight of the fact they are two separate answers. Though they may very well exist complimentary of each other, for most of us, they are two notions independent of each other. "Who are you," can be a twofold answer. There is the idea of whom we know ourselves to be and there's how others define us; the former being the most important for the embarkation in this book. Outside people only get a surface glimpse of who you are. You are the only one who can truly answer the question of who you are. You know what makes you tick, makes you happy, is important to you, etc. Be the definer of who you are, not the one defined by how others see you.

Once you firmly can stand on and by 'who you are, the answer to 'what you want to be' may come more easily. For some, the two go hand-in-hand, but for others, like me, that answer is also twofold. We have dreams of what we want to be in life. We have goals and aspirations for ourselves and we think, 'Yes, this will work!' However, there are always the voices of influence ringing LOUDLY in our minds that we allow to deter us. For many it is our parents, mentors, guardians, etc. who constantly tell us who we are, what they see for us, and what they think will be a good career path. For me, it was my mom. As a child my mother often told me I could be whatever I wanted to be when I grew up. So when I announced in third grade that I was going to be a lawyer that was the career goal she cultivated and nurtured in me. Never mind that I had other things in life that interested me, this is what I was going to be. Do not be confused, my mother was open to many of my ideas for my life, but being a lawyer is what would be pursued. My mother raised me to be an independent thinker who passionately pursues my dreams and goals, but as time has passed, I have learned that you cannot live life to satisfy everyone else. Come the end of the day it is YOUR life and if YOU are not happy with the decisions YOU'VE made NO ONE will be happy with you. I've learned and had to realize the world I live in and the one my mother was brought up in are totally different. We live in a world where we can create our own destiny. We are not confined to what society, or our parents, say we can and/or should be. We are the captains of our own ships! We blaze our own trails! We have our own plans, dreams, goals, hopes, and aspirations for our lives; so why are we sitting and watching life pass us by? Make that personal, why are YOU watching life pass you by trying to live out the dreams of someone else?

As I look back over the many years since these questions were posed to me, I think about where I am in my own life, and the journey that I'm still on, living out the life I have planned for myself. Am I a lawyer yet? No. Am I pursuing what I want to be in life? Yes. What is that? I was reminded not too long ago that we were all created for a purpose. We were designed with all the skills we need to carry out the purpose for which the Creator made us. It matters not your ability, but availability. When you line up with what your purpose is, the doors to pursue it will be opened. I implore you to take heed to the knowledge that is given to you in this book, and stay in tune with YOUR passion, YOUR dreams and YOUR goals.

Kristen Neema Gaither-Thompson
Friend

Authentic \ə-'then-tik\
adjective
- true to one's own personality, spirit, or character

Disclaimer

As you prepare to read this book, there are several important things you should know. The author provides "nuggets that prompt independent thought." The information contained within these pages is actually presented in such a way as to invite readers to assess what is said, mix it with their own intuition, and then develop a truth for themselves. Prescriptive writing would only serve to further infringe upon the readers ability to trust their instincts. Subscribing to this type of behavior would actually run counterproductive to what the book was written to accomplish. Independent Thought.

Preface

When I initially started this book four years ago, I was ready to provide advice to youth and young adults on various areas that I wanted them to be aware of in order to stay true to themselves. But my son, who was nine years old at the time, came in and interrupted me. He could not understand why I was starting to write again so soon. That interruption turned into a journey that I spent watching him growing from a little boy to a young man. I was able to test my assumptions, to see if they would be sound enough to assist a group that I am very passionate about assisting. There were opportunities for me to interact with his growing friendships, coach him in football, teach him in Sunday school, and become immersed in virtually every area of a growing youth's life. Now that I have had the experience, I am in a better position to embark on this journey of assisting 21st century youth and young adults to remain authentic.

In my previous two books, ***Radical Introductions: Beginning by Going Backwards*** and ***Raising a Radical Child***, I discussed how to return to your basic state and begin living a whole, purposeful, and authentic life; and how to raise the children under our influence so they never have to experience a reintroduction themselves.

But as I looked back at the demographic that I had engaged, I realized that I had left an area of opportunity in the demographic that is most vulnerable; young people. So I sat down and started writing again.

Many independent choices are made in our teen and young adult years, away from the safety and comfort of the support structure that we once knew. These choices have a long-lasting impact on who we will become and how we will be perceived in life. The friends we choose, the places we go, and the external resources that we allow to become internal forces, all have bearings on our daily thoughts and actions. So as we walk this walk, I want to suggest a few thoughts that might assist you with being the best you that you can be.

It is my desire to start a revolution and you are at the perfect stage in life to become revolutionaries. This revolution involves remaining true to yourself and embracing your possibilities. It involves creating an atmosphere where you and your peers feel empowered to become trailblazers in this journey of life. It involves not settling for the status quo, but maximizing your position on earth by discovering and walking in purpose. This revolution involves *pursuing your purpose with passion.*

Join me as we celebrate who you were designed to be. The road of life can take you wherever you want it to, but you must first choose the destination; prepare your body, mind, and spirit; and get moving.

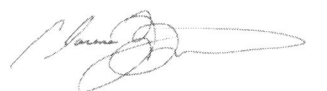

Introduction

Welcome to life. You are entering a new and different stage of living. Your mind is beginning to explore various paths of independence, and you are beginning to test a lot of the assumptions you have made about yourself. This is the very time when you want less guidance and more ownership of your decisions. Therefore, it would seem somewhat of a contradiction that someone needs to invite you to be authentic, because the very nature of authenticity means being truly you. The problem with this is you have spent your entire life being taught to be someone else. Think about the times you wanted to hang out with certain friends and were told you should find a new group to spend time with because, 'birds of a feather flock together,' and the ones you had chosen were described as troublemakers. Or the times you chose to participate in an activity and were told, 'That is not how a young lady/young man acts.' This advice was not given to change you, but to change your actions. However, over the course of your childhood, many instances like these echo in your head and have gently guided you away from the real you, the authentic you.

As you study this book, you will be encouraged to reflect deeply, accept some things you will discover about yourself, and use these things to develop a roadmap for your life. By doing so you will not only be able to successfully express your ambitions to those inquiring, but you will have a guide to keep you steady as you struggle to quiet the wayward noise that tends to draw many off track. During the process of developing this new consciousness, we will also invite you to develop a personal strategic plan that will assist you with broadcasting intelligently to the world what your intentions are, and what, if anything, those who may be interested can do to help facilitate the process. Armed with your map and plan, this book will inspire you with the confidence to remain authentic and invite those around you to do the same.

So, as we begin our journey, take a deep breath, get your highlighter, a pen and pad, and let's get started.

> When you look in the mirror, please understand that you are not a coincidence.

Chapter One

Purpose

"God and Nature first made us what we are, and then out of our own created genius we make ourselves what we want to be. Follow always that great law. Let the sky and God be our limit and Eternity our measurement."

Marcus Garvey

ACKNOWLEDGE

There is a basic fact that you must accept if you are going to benefit from this book and from life. This fact is that we are all created on purpose. Regardless of the circumstances surrounding your upbringing, be they to your satisfaction or not, you have been declared purposed. Medical science will tell you that the race that you won at conception was run by as many as 300 million other competitors. Yet it was you who is reading this book that was birthed on the scene. Even if you take a more detailed look at how you got to be a representative of the human race, you will find that being 1 in 300 million still did not guarantee that you would make it to where you are now. So when you look in the mirror, please understand that you are not a coincidence.

Now, if you are convinced that there is no doubt that you were created on purpose, we are ready to help you to explore why you were created. The truth is, you were not just created on purpose, but you were also created for a specific purpose. You only have to compare you and your best friend's thumbprints to realize that no two people were created alike. And since we are unlike anyone else, our purpose for being created could not possibly be the same as anyone else's. Let's take for example the invention of the brush. Just because they both contain the name brush, doesn't mean you would use a toothbrush and a hairbrush to complete the same task. Likewise, you may look like your siblings, friends, or classmates, but your reason for being created serves a totally different purpose. And for you to become or remain authentic, you will have to discover and adopt that uniqueness.

LIST

If you are not sure of the purpose for which you were created, there are a couple of ways that I can suggest that will provide clues for you. The first way is based on teachings from one of my early role models, Dr. Myles Munroe. Dr. Munroe introduced the first thoughts of purpose to me at an early age, and I have spent the remainder of my life researching, exploring, and refining his teachings in an effort to convince others to live a purposeful life. Some of his points on purpose are:

    1. Everything in life has a purpose.

    2. Not every purpose is known.

3. Where the purpose of a thing is not known, abuse is inevitable. (Guaranteed to happen.)
4. Purpose is the key to fulfillment.
5. Purpose predicts design and design produces potential.
6. Life without purpose is existence without reason.
7. The nature of a thing is the clue to its potential and its purpose.
8. You might not know the purpose of a thing, but if you learn the nature of that thing you can get close.
9. Purpose is always accompanied by certain natural abilities.

Now if we are to use the teachings of Dr. Munroe to look for our purpose, it will call for us to take an introspective look at our lives. Focusing on the final of these nine principles leads us to look at our natural abilities. One of the easiest ways for you to do that would be to make a list of those abilities that come natural to you. To increase the accuracy, I actually ask individuals to make two lists. On the first list, just like above, I ask individuals to write five things that they naturally do well or their strengths. On the second list I ask individuals to write five things they really enjoy doing or their interests. These lists should not focus on things like sports or jobs; they should actually be broken down to their most basic element. For instance if you like basketball, I would ask why you like basketball? Is it because you like to run in short bursts, do you like to jump, do you like team competition, etc.? If it is baby-sitting, is it working with children, caring for the defenseless, etc.? The point is getting to the natural abilities and interests that you have.

I believe you are at a better place to answer these questions than your, parents, guardians or teachers. Because for some reason the older we get, the more we discount our natural abilities and interests. As a matter of fact, adults tend to negotiate in their own minds whether or not to write down on paper those things that come to mind. Please do not fall into this trap of discounting your thoughts and abilities.

Another way you can get a glimpse of your purpose is by taking a look at the things that trouble you. Someone once said, "Your frustration is the key to your allocation." This simply means that if you come across something that irritates you, that irritation is a clear indication of what you have the natural abilities to address. So sit down and give some thought to the things that annoy you. Do you get angry when you see someone mistreat children? Are you infuriated when you hear of injustice to a particular gender, race, or class of people? Is your frustration dealing with miseducation or misinformation? Whatever that thing is that captures your attention and makes your blood boil may just be inviting you to develop a solution to address it. At a minimum that thing will cause you to call upon an ability that you have to temporarily remedy the situation.

Here is the story of how I found my purpose. First of all, there have always been clues, like breadcrumbs, scattered along my life's path. Sometimes these clues caught my attention, but sometimes I was unaware of them. But as I look back over my life now, I can see the patterns that existed. From the activities I participated in, at least the ones that I enjoyed, to the friends I chose. There were even clues in the different duties I sought at my various places of employment. Ultimately it was a clear, audible voice in my head that brought my attention to my purpose.

Years ago, as manager for one of the major discount retailers, I would constantly hear the employees speaking negatively about some of the youth who would come in to apply for jobs. It reminded me of the same conversation I would hear from co-workers at a job I had years before while in college. In both instances the expectation and the reality of employing these youth was negative. In both instances it appeared that the youth lacked some basic exposure and training that, if available to them, would drastically improve their preparation and presence. Though I was at two very different points in my life, held two very different positions in those companies, and these experiences happened in two totally different regions of the country, the situations were virtually the same. So one day as I stood and witnessed a group of young people enter the store and act in a way that supported the stereotype that was placed on them, I said to myself, somebody has to do something. And almost immediately a voice came back and said, "Yes you." After looking around, only to find no one there, I knew my assignment had chosen me. My purpose had been revealed. The ironic thing about this was that the solution would require natural skills, strengths, and abilities that I either already had, or already acquired.

The bottom line is, if you are striving to be the authentic you, the first key is to know your purpose. If you already know and are operating in that purpose, you're ahead of the game. If not and you are interested in finding your purpose, take advantage of the advice offered earlier in this chapter.

> "Ignorance of **PURPOSE** produces abuse of talent."
> Dr. Myles Munroe

> Simply put, the internal compass is the voice in your head that aligns you with your morals, values, and purpose.

Chapter Two

The Internal Compass

"Isn't it strange how much we know if only we ask ourselves instead of somebody else."

Richard Bach

"To thine own self be true." Have you ever heard this phrase and wondered what it meant? Once you understand it and can assign true meaning for it in your life, you will be empowered beyond measure. As a young adult, not too many people will give you a lot of credit for your wisdom, but that is all about to change. When you learn to accept the gift that you were created to be and grow confident with the contribution that you bring to this world, you will begin to speak from a new place. You will show up authentically every time, and the confidence that you show will ensure those you encounter that you are centered, level, and determined. This chapter is designed to introduce you to and get you comfortable with your internal compass. In this case, when you become acquainted with yourself and stay true to yourself, you can then extend this true self to others.

You may have heard words like spirit, consciousness, heart's desire, mind's eye, or internal roadmap used to describe the internal compass. Simply put, the internal compass is the voice in your head that aligns you with your morals, values, and purpose. For instance, have you ever prepared to do something you felt was the right thing for you to do and someone tried to convince you otherwise. No matter how hard they tried to persuade you, something told you what you were thinking was right. That was your internal compass confirming that the path you were attempting to take was indeed in alignment with what you should have been doing. This phenomenon is always happening; it's just that we are not always aware of its operation. Your internal compass was placed into you at conception and was calibrated at the exact moment you were first purposed to exist.

When you accept that you were created for a purpose, the thought of having an internal guide is not so hard to comprehend. Consider that a need existed in this world and you were the answer to its fulfillment. At your point of origin, the Master of the Universe developed every conceivable thing needed to operate in accordance to filling the need and placed it inside of you. Then He sent you armed with a compass and roadmap to walk out that destiny and fulfill the need. The collection of things He placed in you is unique to your situation and no one else's. Fresh out of the birth experience we immediately began to be gently drawn towards the purpose for our creation by many unseen and unknown forces. We are guided on this journey by our internal compass that says yes, no, left, or right for every step of the way. During our daily walk through life, the compass sends us signals to make us aware of whether or not we are aligned correctly with our intended path. This compass is leading us until we get to the point that we recognize and can read our map.

For many of us, the older we get the farther we stray from our preset destination or purpose. This is because we were never taught about the existence or importance of our internal compass. Instead we were taught respect for authority and its wisdom, without regard for the purpose for which we were born. Now don't get me wrong, this was done in an effort to protect us from ourselves; but it is also often done in absence of consulting our own map. Yet this compass has continued to point us towards our destiny. Many times we have not recognized its call, or it has been drowned out by 'grey noise.' Grey noise is advice and commands that have been placed on our lives, sometimes for our good and sometimes to our detriment, by people who have influence over us. Herein lies the source of much of our conflict. We try to adhere to the call of our purpose while also trying to obey the inconsistent mandates that are placed on our lives.

My suggestion is that you take a time-out; identify what your driving forces are, and determine if they are working towards your liberation or away from your destiny. As I mentioned earlier, this is a time in your life when you may be testing your independence. You just want to make sure this independence is not pushing you to a place that is counter-productive to your purpose. Take the time out and do the self-assessment that will allow you to analyze your current state of mind. In gentle silence ask yourself some hard questions regarding your attitude and actions. If the answers are consistent with how you think you should be moving, then great; if not then I invite you to give some thought to how this attitude and these actions can be modified.

The point of this chapter is to realize that we have an internal compass. It is made totally for us, with our destination in mind. This compass only speaks to us and will not necessarily be understood by anyone else. The compass always directs us regardless of whether we listen to it or not. It is aligned with our morals and values, so this compass will never lead us astray. Once we embrace the presence and power of our compass, it will be our source of immeasurable strength, focus, and stability. When others witness our reliance on our internal compass, they will begin to give us credit for our wisdom.

> *"This above all: to thine ownself be true, And it must follow, as the night the day, Thou canst not then be false to any man."*
>
> —Shakespeare-Hamlet

Map Reading Class

As mentioned earlier in the chapter, we are gifted with a compass, but are rarely given a class on map reading. Our compass is a tool used to assist us in navigating our life's map. This map outlines the steps we are to take to reach our destination, our purpose. Unless we take the time to discover and understand our purpose, we will constantly be swayed by everything that looks appealing. Once we get an idea of our purpose then we can start to develop a detailed strategy to reach our destination. As we discussed in the previous chapter, this is best accomplished by developing two lists. To give you a better visual, let's use a simple equation to get started. This equation, Potential + Passion = Purpose, can be used to facilitate the process. 'Potential' represents those things in our life that we do well, or your strengths from the earlier list. These talents will need to be sharpened through formal and/or informal education and exposure, but executing task utilizing them comes easy. 'Passion' represents those things in our life that we truly enjoy doing. These are hobbies and other activities that we allow to consume our free time. Again these are the interests you wrote on the list in the previous chapter. The next step is to study these two lists and begin researching the places—schools, internships, jobs—, which they appear. The results of this research should provide you with a broad area where you should be able to get a good idea for why you were created. Be careful not to focus heavily on any particular job in these areas because doing so will likely prevent you from remaining on purpose. Let me explain this. There will be many industries, jobs, careers, etc., where you will be able to see yourself occupying, but the goal is to adapt an entrepreneurial mindset. As you find areas to connect with your talents, do so with the understanding that your purpose will not change, but the particular areas for the fulfillment of that purpose will. And when that time comes, for you to remain authentic it may be necessary for you to find another area, industry, job, etc., in which to connect your talents. This thinking is different from what many will feel comfortable with, but if you are to remain authentic and always on purpose, understanding this flexibility is crucial. As adults we tend to sell ourselves out and compromise our purpose at the whim of a salary or a title. We get so involved in the mission of the industry that even when the job we were hired to do changes to be something no longer involving things on our list, we adapt for the sake of our perceived job security. The bottom line is this; the purpose for our creation rests in us, and is given for us to service the world and humankind. When we link ourselves to a job, it is to provide that service. The moment we lose sight of this is the moment we began to merge ourselves with someone else's purpose. So embrace the situation by figuring out a way to provide a service, but not to the extent that you are lost to yourself and your purpose.

The final step is to develop a strategy consisting of activities, organizations, and individuals who will be beneficial to your journey. This could be extra-curricular sports, fine arts, and clubs. It can also include finding peer groups, mentors, and role models who understand, support, and/or are headed in the same direction as you.

Now that you have a clearer picture of your map, you must rely on your internal compass and stay the course. What you have discovered should feel natural to you. The area you begin to operate in, the classes you begin to take, the associates that make up your inner circle, should all effortlessly fit you. Your successes will begin mounting, you will stay motivated, and others will recognize your drive. Any time something comes into your life that is inconsistent with your map, you will know immediately. That something won't feel the same, it will knock you off balance, and it will drain your energy. When this happens you must stop immediately and consult your inner compass, spirit, or consciousness. If this mechanism verifies this thing as a distraction, you must get it out of your life, no matter what or who it may be.

When you consistently live at the level of consulting your internal compass, your confidence will grow immensely. You will truly begin to KNOW THINE SELF, and to THINE OWN SELF live true, authentically, and fulfilled.

Chapter Three

Choices

"You can choose your choices, but you cannot choose your consequences."

Larry Williams

One thing we possess that no one will ever be able to take away from us is our ability to choose. From the outset this may not seem true, but think about it for a minute. Even if the consequence that results from that choice is not what we desire, we still have the ability to choose. You can choose to ignore the sign on the door that says out, but it doesn't mean the door will open for you when you approach. Or you can choose to try and utilize your cell phone even though you have no signal and no call will be made, but that still does not take away the choice you have. In this chapter what we will be doing is assisting you with developing a strategy so you will always (a) understand your choices; (b) evaluate your choices with ease; and (c) ensure that your choice aligns with your internal compass.

Believe it or not, our upbringing plays a tremendous role in the choices we make. Early in life we begin to pattern our decisions to create an environment consistent with the way we view the world. The issue with this approach is that this view is oftentimes influenced by the decisions others have made, which may or may not work to our advantage. Beyond this, we make choices we feel will lead to a harmonious balance with the people in our lives, regardless of the stripping away of our personal desires. Think about the times you have chosen to agree to do something or take on a responsibility you were not interested in or did not understand. In an effort to maintain a positive relationship or image, you did it anyway. When you completed the action you did not get the feedback you were anticipating from the person who asked you to do it, so you felt a little deflated and were perhaps ridiculed for not meeting expectations. If we really look at this situation, what we would discover is that the very moment you decided to ignore your feelings and consent to the feelings of the person asking you to do the task, you were choosing to fully accept the consequences of those actions. Conversely, had you decided to decline the request, you would have been choosing to fully accept the consequence of the requester's response to this denial. The good thing about the second decision is that the result is the product of being authentic, and therefore the outcome is one we should be more willing to accept. In most cases we feel set-up by the request and unfortunately people can ask of us what they please. It is our responsibility to only accept doing those things for which we do not mind bearing the consequences.

Let's take a look at our ability to choose when instructed by adults or those who have authority over us. Several years ago I attended a training seminar where the instructor made the statement that "we are always at choice." The instructor went on to explain that no matter what we were faced with, we had the obligation to choose our actions. Then the instructor gave an example using our job, and being given an unethical task by the supervisor. The instructor explained that though our choosing not to follow our supervisor's directive would not be looked upon favorably and we would risk being fired, it did not change the fact that we had a choice in the matter. Our choices consisted of **a)** maintaining allegiance to our company, even though our actions would be dishonorable, or **b)** choosing to maintain integrity and consequently choosing to no longer remain employed at a company that would force its employees to participate in questionable activities. If we were to carry this example further, we would also recognize that our supervisor, too, had some choices to make. They could **a)** reevaluate the task they assigned and decide that our noncompliance was not out of disrespect and retract the assignment, or **b)** choose to maintain their insistence upon our completing the task and upon our continual noncompliance, terminate our employment. But then this leaves us with more choices. We can **a)** choose to accept the dismissal quietly and move on with our life, or **b)** choose to file a grievance or pursue legal action. This in turn gives the company an opportunity to choose. I think you get the idea. We are always at choice.

What happens if the scenario above dealt with a parent or teacher? First of all, you still exist in choice; however, my suggestion would be that you take the opportunity to respectfully discuss the request, your feelings, and your impending choice, with the parent or teacher. We all know just because our parent or caregiver asks us to do something doesn't mean we do it; we just choose not to do it when we think they won't find out. But imagine the maturity you will begin to show when you begin to logically develop your choices and articulate them with respect. Take for instance the teacher who wants you to volunteer for an organization or program that you do not like. The way you react or respond to this request could affect your remaining time at this school or in the teacher's class. Your first choice could be to simply comply with the teacher's wishes and make yourself miserable; or the second choice is to not comply and face being rejected. This typically represents the extent of the choices we see, but let's look at a third option called compromise. In this situation imagine what would happen if you took the time to look at it from the teacher's perspective. Consider the best things that could happen if you participated in the endeavor **(Pros)**, and then consider the worst **(Cons)**. Next consider the main reason why you are in opposition to participating in the endeavor **(Discriminator)**. Something that often helps me is a pros and cons chart. **(See end of chapter)**. Now, from a neutral position, choose which decision will serve you best. If you choose not to accept the teacher's invitation to participate, you are suddenly in an educated position to articulate why you think differently than they do. And though the teacher may not agree with your decision, they should certainly appreciate the fact that you arrived at your decision through an informed process.

When dealing with parents, caregivers, or other adults who have influence over you, the same process should apply. Though they are asking you to do something that you don't understand at the time, chances are they have gone through the process of making sure the request at least makes sense to them. If you are to gain any respect for your decision and independence, it will only come when you can show that your decision comes from an equally thought out position. Though you are ultimately responsible for the consequence of your choice, your parent or caregiver is trying to guide your choice so that you will receive the minimum exposure to risk, and maximum benefit. With that being said, your agenda should be to show that through your thought process you have considered those two elements and many more.

To give you an example, I recently learned of a young man who was participating in an out-of-town school trip. In route to their final destination, the school official decided to stop at a shopping mall and give the students some free time. At that very moment, the official **chose** to allow the students to be responsible for their own actions, as opposed to chaperoning or hovering over the students. At some time during the short stop, one of the students made a **choice** to take something that did not belong to them. The consequence of that choice was to be arrested, embarrassed, and taken to jail. The consequence of the school official's choice was being embarrassed, having to inform the student's parents of their child's arrest, and having to explain to their supervisor why the students were not accompanied at all times and how the incident occurred.

In the above example two people had and made choices, and both experienced negative consequences. Therefore, in the future, the school official, the student's parents, and the official's supervisor will probably all **choose** to maintain more control over the students in areas where they can minimize the unsafe **choices** that are available for them to make. The point I want you to walk away with is that, if you cannot assure the people who have influence over you that you can make well thought out **choices**, they will probably attempt to minimize the harmful **choices** you are able to make.

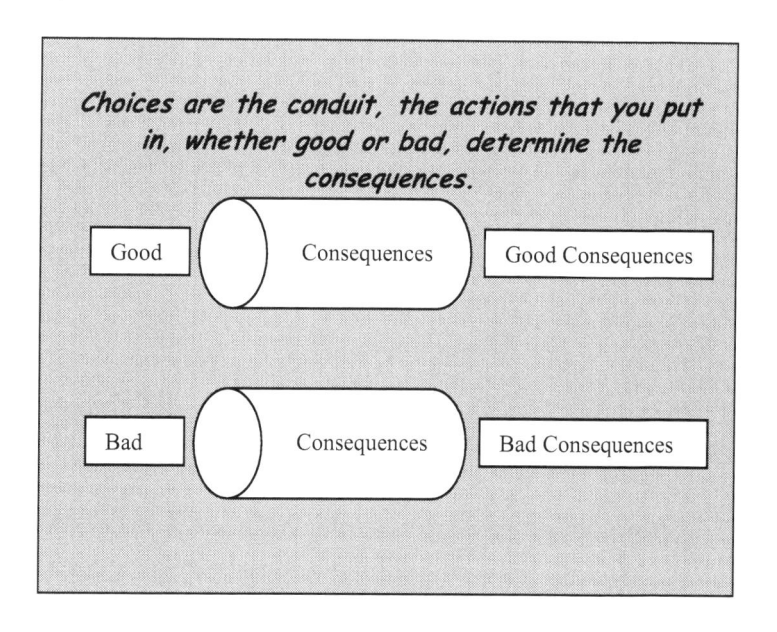

Choices are the conduit, the actions that you put in, whether good or bad, determine the consequences.

| Good | Consequences | Good Consequences |
| Bad | Consequences | Bad Consequences |

The older you get, the more impact the choices you make have on your life. As you approach the end of your high school years and into college, the things that you do start a rippling effect. If you begin sowing good choices then you will begin to see good things happening in your life. Consequently if the actions and activities you participate in are negative, you'll begin experiencing difficulty accomplishing many of the goals you have set for yourself. So as you spend time thinking, planning, and setting goals, also take the time to think about questionable choices that you have made or have thought about making that will hinder your progress in those areas.

Every day while going to school, going to work, or responding to teachers, family, and friends, take a little extra time to evaluate the pros and cons of every decision you are faced with, no matter how small. Then practice making choices not based on the immediate gratification you may receive, but base them on the possible, long-lasting consequences of that decision. What you will find in many cases is that your view will be different. And as you begin making more choices based on how they may affect your future as opposed to how they make you feel today, you will discover that the consequences of your actions will far exceed any accomplishment you will have experienced from a less informed position. Plus you will feel more empowered and emboldened to articulate your desires to those who are in opposition to your choices.

At the end of this chapter you will find a decision matrix that can be used to make informed choices. After you spend a little time using this tool, the concept will become familiar to you. At that point you should be able to visualize the box and make choices with greater ease. The PROS box is used to jot down the positive aspects of the decision. The CONS box is used to jot down the negative aspects of your decision. The Discriminators box is used to write down any other information that may be useful in helping you make a decision. For example, say you are trying to decide whether to take a bus or a cab. You are leaning toward taking the bus, so here is how the matrix may help.

PROS	CONS
Bus is cheaper	I have to walk 10 blocks to get home from the stop
Bus comes faster	It is late at night
	I am alone

Discriminators: I don't have enough money for the cab and I have a personal protection device.

If you were making a decision based on the above matrix, you would probably stick with your decision to ride the bus. If discriminators were different, let's say your roommate, neighbor, or parent would loan you the money when you got home, you would probably opt to take the cab rather than risk taking the bus under the circumstances. So now that you see how to complete the matrix use it at your leisure to make daily decisions.

Decision Matrix

PROS	CONS

Discriminators:

> First of all we should always strive to surround ourselves with like-minded, like-performing individuals.

Chapter Four

Gravitate

"No man is an island, Entire of itself."
John Donne

The thought behind gravitate is to gravitate toward assets and not liabilities. In your quest for authenticity, there will be many times where you will reach a crossroad and have to call upon your decision-making skills. Everything that is good *to* you is not always good *for* you, so do whatever possible to surround yourself with people and participate in activities that will support you and your growth. This chapter will give you a few things to consider.

Misery Lovers

You may have heard the saying "misery loves company," but have you ever sat back and thought about what it means. As we have discussed before, 'birds of a feather flock together,' but when a bird is alone and wallowing in self-pity, it looks for someone to share their pain. Have you ever noticed that your peers will often invite you to take part in reckless or unproductive activities, but will rarely invite you to take part in worthwhile pursuits? Classmates or friends will be more likely to invite you to sneak out or stay out past curfew to attend a party, but chances are they will not look for you when they are headed to a tutoring session or to the library. Why do you think it is easier to participate in or invite someone to participate in unproductive activities rather than beneficial ones? Is it because we think we will be seen as cool or hip if we participate in these types of activities but will be seen as odd or square if we are seen participating in positive, life-building activities? Or do we simply want to bring others *down* to our level but see less benefit in pulling them *up* to our level?

What about the peer who becomes bitter from their interaction with a person or group of people; the fellow student who does not care for a particular teacher; or the co-worker who has had a run-in with the boss. Why is it that they always search out someone to share in their pity-party? Life tends to bring to us what we are searching for; consequently, if we search for misery, misery is what we will find. If you are to remain authentic, you should avoid people who change your state of mind for the worse, and find and gravitate towards those individuals who want to lift you up or accompany you to higher heights.

Herd Growing

Never become the strongest buffalo in the herd. It is said that the weakest buffalo in a herd is the first and easiest to be hunted down and killed. But there is an equally troubling problem when you become the strongest buffalo in the herd.

First of all we should always strive to surround ourselves with like-minded, like-performing individuals. The goal is to make this group one that constantly strives to increase their mental and social capacity. There should either be a constant rotation of leaders, or when the group gets to the point where it is stagnant it should seek to add a stronger member to its ranks. This way the group will always strive to move forward. Once you become the strongest person in your group, you will have the tendency to relax and not push as hard because you have no one to overtake. New leadership, in this case, will ensure new ideas, new challenges, and new successes.

As your core group becomes recognized as one that continuously strives for excellence, you will attract other individuals who are eager to become a part. While in most cases this will be a positive thing, it does not always work this way. Be sure that you are constantly monitoring to weed out misery-lovers and freeloaders. If you are to remain authentic, each member of the herd has to know their purpose and supplement other members of the herd as well.

> *"Misery loves company."*

Extra-curricular Activities

How do you choose the activities in which you participate? Do you find what is most popular and sign up? Do you follow what a friend is doing? Do you listen to what others tell you that you should be good at? These are some of the ways most people will choose their activities, but not you. Being authentic means consulting your *Internal Compass*.

It can be very easy to fall into the trap of, 'you are so tall, you need to be playing basketball,' 'you are so fast, you need to be running track,' or 'you are so pretty or handsome, you need to be a model.' But do those activities really support your purpose? Yes you have been given your natural abilities and attributes to use, but it does not mean that your talents are to be pigeonholed. There may be some activity that has not been identified that may serve you better. This is not to say that you cannot or should not participate in a popular activity. I am only inviting you to consider activities that truly take into account the reason for which you were created. It is great to have a musical ear, but it is a waste of your time, your band or orchestra's time, and your band director or conductor's time, if you are not passionate about the activity and willing to put in the time to practice and improve on your talent. What I am really saying is to spend your time on those activities that support your purpose and for which you will be willing to consistently give 100%.

Education

What I am about to discuss with you is a very sensitive subject, but it is too important to leave out. It really bothers me to think of the amount of money and time individuals spend on education without aligning it with their authenticity. I do support educating oneself. However, it is equally important to do so only as it pertains to pursuing your purpose. Just as you seek to participate only in extra-curricular activities that support you, it is important to take those classes, pursue those degrees, and participate in certification programs that support your growth. Even if you are in high school there is a flexibility that will allow you to choose some classes that support your authenticity. In college there is the major and minor you choose as well as the electives that are offered that allow you to customize your path.

Do not be tempted to just get the schooling. Please go for the learning that will support you, your purpose, and your path. Do this even at the expense of isolating yourself from some who may think they know what is better for you. I am not suggesting that you be rude or disrespectful. However, I am suggesting that you get a firm hold on your purpose and those things it will take for you to fulfill it, and pursue them as if your life depends on it, because it does. If you choose college, have a detailed plan for attending and a clear idea of how you will utilize the information learned. If you continue on to get your master's degree, Ph.D., M.D., etc., it is important that you know what is in it for you. Because at the end of the day, if it does not produce what others have led you to believe it should, you will still know what you have gotten from it, and you will be satisfied.

With all this information it is clear that you need to gravitate towards people and activities that support your growth. Once you have gone through the process of discovering your purpose, it is crucial that you participate as much as possible in things and with people who will keep you connected to that purpose. In life, there is never a shortage of distractions to pull us from our path, so the goal is to do all that is necessary to eliminate those diversions. If you find yourself in a crowd or group whose purpose does not support yours, you will only be drawn off track.

It is alarming the number of individuals who late in life rediscover a passion that they had when they were young. When they look back on it, they often realize that they allowed some activities or people to lead them away from their true passion. The sad part is, oftentimes the replacement person or activity only held their attention for a short while, but by the time they realized it, it was too late to go back. Do not allow this to happen to you. Remain authentic and surround yourself with friends, mentors, projects, programs, and activities that support your growth.

Chapter Five

Tic-Toc, Tic-Toc, Life-Clock

*"Ooh, in time it could have been so much more
The time is precious I know
In time it could have been so much more
The time has nothing to show"*
Boy George and the Culture Club

Are you really ready for what life has to offer? Have you been preparing yourself for the moment that all of your decisions matter; the time when your decisions count for or against the balance in the bank account life has given you? Well I have news for you; the withdrawals have already begun.

Some years ago I had a conversation with one of my nieces and her college friend. In the conversation I discovered that they felt as though they had until the end of their college careers to make productive decisions, and when that time came that they had an infinite amount of do-overs. Do you feel this way too? If so, I have some bad news for you. Every decision you have made to this point in your life has an affect on the rest of your life. This is why I have expressed the importance of discovering your purpose *now*.

In an earlier chapter we talked about choices. Take some time and think about what we discussed in that chapter. We gave you an illustration that showed that all consequences follow what we assign to them. If our actions are positive, so are our consequences. If our actions are negative, so are our consequences. If our actions are neutral, well then so are our consequences. This is what happens when we just go with the flow, allowing life to make choices for us. We have to accept whatever consequences the moment assigns. If we are to lead a truly authentic and purpose-filled life, we have to make our assignments with purpose. Leave nothing to chance.

> *Assign: To set aside for a particular purpose.*

Every hour, day, week, month, or year that we do not assign what we want is a waste of our precious time. Our average life span is 78.2 years. So let's say that you expect to live 80 years. That will give you approximately 29,219 days to accomplish everything you want and need to in your lifetime. Now at first look this seems to be a lot of time on your hands, but how old are you right now? Just say that you are 20 years old as you read this book; that was the age of my niece and her friend. You have already gone through a fourth of your life without assigning your actions according to your purpose. Based on the consequences of your neutral or negative choices, you will either end up initially following a path that is not aligned with your purpose, or spend the next few years retooling or retraining yourself according to your purpose. If you go with continuing to follow your current path, which most will do because it is familiar and they are already well under way, it will take you 15 to 20 years to decide that you have not ended up where you are purposed to be; especially if you have already begun to pursue a college degree, entered the military, or started working. This scenario just took another fourth of your life. Now instead of the 29,000 plus days you started with, you have about 14,610 days left to discover, prepare for, and pursue your purpose. Add a family and responsibility into the equation and it seriously diminishes the amount of time it will take you to pursue that purpose.

The illustration above may seem far-fetched, but just take a poll of adults that you know. You only need ask them two questions: How old are you, and are you pursuing or operating in your purpose? What you will find is that many of them have not even taken the time to even discover their purpose. For that group I wrote my first book, *Radical Introductions; Beginning By Going Backwards*. I wrote this book for you with the hope that you will never have to read the first one.

If you are to remain authentic, as this book advocates, it is imperative that you not make the mistake of putting off making productive decisions. Going back to the scenario we discussed above, if instead of continuing down the easy, familiar path, stop. Assess your purpose and apply it to every decision you make, activity you participate in, and friend or acquaintance you accept into your life, your purpose-filled years will increase dramatically. Instead of the 15 to 20 years you spend trying to find yourself through climbing the corporate ladder or searching for arbitrary certifications and accolades, you can take two to three years discovering and operating on purpose. Instead of having less than 15,000 days, you now have over 20,000 days to enjoy and operate authentically.

The point I am trying to make is that you are already at the stage where your decisions count toward a productive life. The clock is ticking and how you fill that time is up to you. Every decision we make, even including the boyfriend or girlfriend you choose for yourself, determines how you spend your time. Do not waste what little precious time you have making decisions that do not add to the final result you want for your life. Because, honestly, no one knows how much time they truly have on earth. To further imprint this thought in your mind, I will leave you with a visual. Imagine that at birth we were all given a candle. This candle, though it resembles other candles, has its own rate of burning. As soon as we began to breathe, this candle was lit. Every day of our life, this candle burns until it finally burns out. No amount of hoping, wishing, or begging will add to the wax on this candle. When it is finished, it is finished. Please don't waste your wax on things that do not matter, or you will not leave the aroma and the light that you were created to leave.

> Never Compromise for friends.
> Never Compromise for fame.
> Never Compromise for fortune.

Chapter Six

Never Compromise

"It takes courage to grow up and become who you really are."
e.e. cummings

Compromise is what we do when we are not firm on our convictions. If you have gone through this book and understood and accepted the concepts you have read, compromise is the last thing you would want to consider. This does not mean you should constantly reevaluate your position based on new or relevant information. What we are saying here is that you should not give up your convictions based on information or individuals who do not consider your purpose or lists.

The concept ALIGN, which I have laced throughout this book and I tour the country presenting in workshops, uses NEVER COMPROMISE as its final pillar. The way I present it is by saying, '*Never Compromise* for friends, fame, or fortune.' The reason it is presented this way is because these are typically the three reasons we compromise on our dreams. So we will take the opportunity to discuss these areas one by one.

Never Compromise for friends. In earlier chapters you have been advised against surrounding yourself with those who love misery; encouraged to select a growing and productive herd; and told about the importance of the mate you choose. You must eliminate unnecessary distractions and these suggestions are ways to do so. It is hard enough to develop your list, meditate, set a path for your life, and begin to walk in that direction. If those people who you are close to or trust become an obstacle, continuing on your journey becomes almost impossible. Even though these individuals may mean well, if they do not consider your lists or your purpose, they have no way of assuring they are giving you relevant or sufficient advice. Even if you are given the best advice from the best source, you are not guaranteed to secure the success that they have achieved. The reason is because without considering your starting point and the tools you have to work with, there is no way to predict where you will end up. So please do not compromise for friends. Stick to the path you have been created for based on your internal compass and roadmap.

Never Compromise for fame. What is fame anyway? Is it to be known by the masses? Is it to become a household name? Is it to have the paparazzi flashing photographs all day and night? Or do you consider it gaining the respect of your peers? Regardless of how you define fame, imagine achieving it by pretending to be something you are not. Imagine giving up on your path to seek out immediate gratification and instant celebrity. Imagine gaining a reputation of being someone who you do not even recognize when you are alone. This will not keep you happy and it will not allow you to be authentic. When we do not take the opportunity to discover the gifts we are given and the areas in which they can be put to best use, but rather allow other things and pursuits to shape our life, we make a grave mistake. We build a façade that we will have to go through a great deal of trouble to maintain. Think about the artist who enters the profession because they wanted to make a difference by delivering a particular type of message, but once in the business, this artist realizes it is more profitable and acceptable to lay aside their message for a more commercially appealing one. They may rise to the top quickly, but eventually this compromise will begin to wear on them, or they will begin doing things to numb the feeling or blind them to their current reality. Many musical artists have lost their voices and their way by compromising their message for instant fame. They then find themselves dropping out of the limelight prematurely or turning to drugs and/or alcohol to dull the ache of becoming a sell-out. So please do not compromise for fame. To do so leads to a slippery slope that may not provide a good return on your investment.

Never Compromise for fortune. There is a biblical scripture that says, *'For the love of money is the root of all evils.'* This is not to say we are not to make money or have a financial goal. It is more about not letting money be your motivation. The reality is we should expect to be compensated for the talents and change we bring to the world, but it is our responsibility to perfect these talents and be true to them. When we make money our focus we tend to compromise on things that may otherwise be important to us. No amount of money will ever be enough when money is the thing we seek. And when we run out of productive ways to make money we will begin seeking alternatives. I recently read of a wealthy man who said that every morning he wakes up and is not on the list of the richest people alive, he has to go to work. If this motivates you to work harder and stay the course of your purpose, it can yield good results. But if it causes you to change paths in an effort to find a way to make more money, it is usually a major mistake and one that will eventually cost more than a person could ever gain. So finally, please do not compromise for fortune. If you cannot make a good living doing what you love, the money will cause you more heartache than you will be able to afford.

You are well on your way to success and happiness if you stay the course of your creation and convictions. But the moment you decide to lay these aside for anything that is not consistent with what you are purposed to become, you lose your authenticity. Consider your life a masterpiece that is being painted by a true artist. As long as the canvas remains in the hands, mind, and control of the artist, it is invaluable. However, the moment that it is under the influence and control of another, it is no longer priceless. If you do not believe this, try passing off a counterfeit for a work by Monet or Leonardo da Vinci and see the results. A gentleman in Alexandria, LA, found out in 2011 when he received a punishment of 25 months in prison and $327,000. Then there is the auction house that was fined $4,800,000 for selling a counterfeit picture to a member of the Russian Government. Never Compromise the authentic you for the counterfeit someone else. It will not be worth it in the end.

> Maintain the lines of communication with your internal compass, as it will guide you places about which you have only dreamed.

Conclusion

Well here we are at the end, or perhaps the beginning, of your journey to authenticity. In this book we have shared some practical information aimed at helping you discover your internal design. Maintain the lines of communication with your internal compass, as it will guide you places about which you have only dreamed. After all, that compass helped to manufacture those dreams. The more acquainted you become with your authentic self and the more you utilize your roadmap, the easier you will find the road ahead and the more comfortable you will be with the choices you make. You will feel like your life really fits you, and it does, because it was designed that way.

My non-profit organization On Your Purpose, Inc., facilitates monthly public seminars designed to walk individuals through the process of discovering their purpose and developing a personal strategic plan for their life (www.alignmentseminar.com). Once attendees complete their lists, we ask them to meditate on them and then put some concrete things into place to get them started and keep them operating in purpose. This would be a great opportunity for you to do the same thing. Start by writing at least two goals for your authentic life. Once you have completed your two goals, develop at least two objectives for each goal. Finally, assign three activities for each of your objectives, starting with something you can began today. A sample of one of my goals, objectives, and activities can be found at the end of the chapter. This will give you written direction as you live your authentic life. As you accomplish your goals, repeat the process, each time consulting your lists and your internal compass.

Thank you for striving to be your authentic self. Now go out and share this information with your family and friends. Taking the step to authenticity is truly liberating and once you live this way, you want others to be freed up to live this way as well.

Sample Goal, Objectives and Activities

Goal: To compel individuals to follow their purpose by encouraging them to trust and think for themselves.

Objectives:
1. I will invite the general public to at least one seminar per month for the next 12 months.
2. I will engage at least 100 individuals on the topic of purpose and their future plans by August 15, 2013.

Activities:

1. Research and secure locations available for hosting seminars.

2. Develop marketing materials and distribute through print, electronic, and social media.

3. Develop workshop content, handouts, etc., to be used for seminars.

Clarence T. Brown

Clarence T. Brown specializes in ALIGNment, a Five-Step process of calibrating your internal and external resources to maximize performance. Through speaking, training, consulting, and writing, he uses his more than 15 years of for-profit and non-profit management experience to assist clients with ALIGNing their mission with their resources. As founder of The Talking Bout, LLC, Brown uses a unique perspective and a thought- provoking approach to develop trainings and keynote speeches to exceed his customers' needs.

Brown also leads a non-profit organization, On Your Purpose, Inc., whose mission is to provide educational and motivational seminars for youth and young adults. This organization is designed to fill a void that K-12 schools and colleges either do not or cannot fill.

Clarence T. Brown is a native of Augusta, GA and is married to his high school sweetheart, Consuela. He also has one son, Clarence III, and currently resides in the Washington, DC Metropolitan area.

'Being Authentically Me'
–Clarence T. Brown

Additional Publications

Radical Introduction: Beginning By Going Backwards
-Target Audience (Seasoned Adult)
Order:
http://www.clarencetbrown.com/store.php

Raising A Radical Child
-Target Audience (Parent/Guardian/Mentor)
Order:
http://www.clarencetbrown.com/store.php

Blogs From The Outer Space
- Target Age (All Audiences)
Order:
http://www.clarencetbrown.com/store.php

Also at Amazon.com

Made in the USA
Charleston, SC
24 May 2013